# *What is Peace?*

## *A Discovery of the Many Biblical Facets of Peace*

Rev. Dr. Matthew Webster

# Table of Contents

# Chapter 1 "Peace Be With You"

One of the things that you may not be aware of is that your life is at war. Every day you participate in a spiritual battle and one of the important elements of our life that can suffer or be strengthened as a result of our time spent with the Savior is our peace. It is not that you no will no longer have the peace that Jesus has given you, it is just that depending upon the things that happen to us, the enemy would like to rob us of our peace. So, I wanted to bring peace into your life as we look at what God's Word says about peace starting with the phrase "peace be with you".

In Genesis, Judges, Mark, Luke, 2 Corinthians, Philippians 2 Thessalonians, 1 Timothy, 1 Peter, 2 and 3 John there is this statement used, "peace be with you". What I would like to know is what exactly is peace if it is so important to use in a phrase toward others? Before we start exploring the Biblical definition- how would you define peace?

_______________________________________

_______________________________________

_______________________________________

2 Thessalonians 1:2 says:

"Grace and peace to you from God the Father and the Lord Jesus Christ."

Before we get to the first facet/definition of peace we have to start with grace. **I believe it is grace that leads to peace. Until we know grace, we can't experience peace.**

J. Hampton Keathley III says, "Grace, one might say, is the work of God for man and encompasses everything we receive from God."[1] This would include peace.

Grace (charis) -that which affords joy, pleasure, delight, sweetness, charm, loveliness.

The focus is on the unmerited blessings given to believers in Christ. Through God's marvelous grace, sinners are delivered from their sins and brought into a saving relationship with a holy God, by the work of God on their behalf completely free of charge. Because of this work of God, a believer is given access to real peace.

---

[1] J. Hampton Keathley III. https://bible.org/article/grace-and-peace

This grace does not cease with salvation from sin's penalty but continues as the foundation of the believer's life with God throughout all eternity. These blessings of grace, Paul desires for his readers to experience.

Missionary Don Richardson who served for many years among the primitive tribes in Papua New Guinea wrote a book entitled "The Peace Child." He tells the story of two tribes in Papua New Guinea who maintained a blood feud between themselves for several generations. Each generation fought and nursed their wounds only to fight again killing and maiming more and more people. After years of struggle, the two tribes realized that they must stop fighting or nothing would be left of their peoples. But what could they do to end years of warring between the two tribes?

Don Richardson goes on to tell that the chiefs of the two tribes came together and brought with them a child they called "the peace child". This child was the son of one of the opposing chiefs who was adopted into the family of the opposing chief.

As long as that child lived the two chiefs promised to cease their fighting so that all could live. Richardson had finally found a perfect picture of God's love for us in sending His Son, the Prince of Peace to die for us.[2]

Grace carries with it peace. So, what is peace?

Peace has so many different facets to it. We will explore those different facets in every chapter of this book. To begin with, we will look at a common usage of peace that we will label as facet number one.

Peace Facet #1
Eirene (peace): security, safety, prosperity.

The recent coronavirus pandemic threatened our peace in the world. It doesn't matter where you live you were aware of the virus and to some degree, your level of peace was affected at various points and various times. Security, safety, and prosperity were hard to find words in the news and on the television.

---

[2] https://www.family-times.net/illustration/Peace/201922/.

Every-day tasks like going to the grocery store became stress-filled for our family. When we would listen to the news, it would cause us to wonder how long the quarantine would last and what else we should do to protect our family. There wasn't much peace to be found especially when using the definition of security, safety, prosperity.

Our peace is at stake as the enemy gets us to focus on our situation instead of our position in Christ, that we have the salvation of the Lord. I am not just referring to everlasting life but also physical salvation as well. When the Coronavirus pandemic hit, our spiritual/eternal salvation wasn't our concern. It was our physical salvation, (our security, safety, and prosperity), with the pay cuts, and the job lay-offs that threatened our peace.

**If grace leads to our peace than peace keeps what grace gives.**

The testimony I have is that as I received God's grace, God used the coronavirus to raise my contentment level.

Doesn't that sound strange? I had a routine and a rhythm to my life that was interrupted. No sports, limited appointments to keep, my soul was quieted and my prayer life strengthened. Quality family time rose, my grace level was filled and so my peace started abounding.

**Grace and Peace cannot be manufactured, it comes from God (2 Thessalonians 1:2).**

"Grace and peace to you from God the Father and the Lord Jesus Christ."

**The Greek word for "from" is (apo) and it means of origin of a cause. This means God is the cause and source of my life's peace.**

I don't want to breeze by the simplicity and yet the profoundness of that statement. There is no life circumstance that I could face (good or bad) that could be the source of my life's peace. We may be fooled by our emotions to believe that good times produce peace and bad times simply don't. That's not true.

Our life's peace comes from God, so that in all things, whatever may come, we can have peace. Because God is our source of it.

Many years ago, I served on staff at a church who had the vision to share the congregation's individual stories of unique ways they experienced God. The entire staff decided the best way to do this was to hire a professional photographer to come in and take pictures of different individuals whose stories were hand-picked to be displayed as life-sized posters mounted in our community room.

The photographer did an excellent job as the posters were bright and beautiful and captured your eye. I would watch as community members would be drawn to the life-sized posters and the messages that were written on it from members of their community.

One poster in particular, I wish I could go back and modify the story. The reason for the needed change ties into this verse about God being the cause and source of my life's peace.

I don't remember exactly what the poster said, but it was something like this: "When I am out in nature I am at peace and it makes me want to worship God."
This person's thoughts and experience were authentic and they were not wrong. I have heard countless people say they have been awe-struck by the beauty of God's creation that inspires them to worship. The only problem with this poster is that they need to flip the order of things. It isn't God's creation that gives them peace, it is God himself. Did peace come because of the beauty around them or did peace come in their time of worshipping God and receiving His grace in their lives?

You see nature was a tool that led to praise, but the source of peace is God himself. So, whatever your inspiring place is to worship and spent time with God, go there, and go there often.

In the Old Testament times, they would pray in what was known as secret places to pray (Matthew 6:6).

Every Jewish house had a place for secret devotion. The roofs of their houses were flat places, well adapted for walking, conversation, and meditation (read Bible commentary on Matthew 9:2). Professor Hackett ("*Illustrations of Scripture*," p. 82) says: "On the roof of the house in which I lodged at Damascus were chambers and rooms along the side and at the corners of the open space or terrace, which constitutes often a sort of upper story. I observed the same thing in connection with other houses." Over the porch, or entrance of the house, there was frequently a small room of the size of the porch, raised a story above the rest of the house, expressly appropriated for the place of retirement. Here, in secrecy and solitude, the pious Jew might offer his prayers, unseen by any but the Searcher of hearts. To this place, or some similar place, our Savior directed His disciples to repair when they wished to hold communion with God. This is the place commonly mentioned in the New Testament as the "upper room," or the place for secret prayer.[3]

---

[3] Albert Barnes Notes on the Whole Bible.
https://www.studylight.org/commentary/matthew/6-6.html

The spot that you choose to get away and spent time with God does not matter. It could be the bathroom if you are a parent because it is the only place you can find to be alone with God.
For me often it's the shower. My time in the shower is peaceful where praise happens but the shower itself is not my peacemaker. The place of prayer is a space that allows one the opportunity to spend time with the One who wants to fill us with His peace.

Peter will begin both of his letters in the same way, "May grace and peace be multiplied to you." The verb behind be multiplied is used twelve times in the New Testament and always means increase. To move from lesser to greater.

**It is important to know that both grace and peace can be increased in your life (1 Peter 1:2, 2 Peter 1:2).**

I remember several years ago I was on a vacation with my family in Florida. We had just settled into the condo we were staying and I can tell you that my grace and peace level was low. Traveling in general, especially with children, is an all-out war against my peace. There are also places that we go that we know in advance are peace zappers; the Secretary of State's office, the airport, any mass transit system, doctor's appointments. I hadn't even unpacked yet when my phone rang. There was an individual from the church whose spouse had just died. I was blessed to be able to minister to them on the phone for quite some time. I share this story to say that there will be times when your peace meter hits all-time lows. Life happens. Before you get a chance to unpack the stress, something or someone needs your attention and then your peace sinks even lower.

Peter desires that both grace and peace be multiplied unto us. New measures of both for new moments. Could you go for some more grace and peace in your life? I know I always could. How do we receive more grace and peace?

**God's Word tells us that when you receive revelation in the knowledge of Jesus, it will cause grace and peace to be multiplied in your life (2 Peter 1:2).**

It will cause you to receive all things that pertain to life and godliness.

The more we learn of the beauty and love of our Lord Jesus, the more we see His perfect work on the cross, the more we position ourselves to receive a multiplication of God's grace in our lives.

The peace of God sets our hearts free from fear, stress, worries, anxieties, and cares. Wouldn't you want to have the peace of God presiding over your heart always?

God's divine power has given us all things that pertain not just to godliness, but life as well. Wouldn't you say that health, finances, a good job that glorifies God, and a stable dwelling for your family pertain to life? Well, all these things and everything else which God has already given are released to you through the knowledge of Jesus our Lord.

Let's ask God every day, "Father, give me wisdom and revelation in the knowledge of

Jesus." For to know Jesus is to have grace and peace multiplied to us. To know Jesus is to receive all things pertaining to life and godliness!

After ministering to the man whose wife had died, I ended the conversation and decided to gather with my family at the pool to bask in the warm sun and spend time with God allowing Him to take the stress from the travel and ministry demands away.
You won't always have a nice pool to retreat to or a warm sunny day but it isn't the place, it is the person of Jesus that multiplies unto us His grace and His peace. Find a space to receive more grace and peace in your life. There is always more grace and more joy to be received. We could always use more.

**The good news is when Paul would write grace and peace to you- the word "to you" implies movement. Grace and peace are on the way. More is coming.**

God continues to send you exactly what you need. What an awesome Father.
That's the best father there is. He is so far ahead of us, but also with us, and He is ready to give you more and more of His grace and His peace.

"We ought always to thank God for you, brothers and sisters, and rightly so, because your faith is growing more and more, and the love all of you have for one another is increasing" (2 Thessalonians 1:3).
The first thing that Paul goes to after writing about his desire for their grace and peace to come from God is he models how that might come about as He gives God thanks. In this case, his thanksgiving is for the Christian brothers and sisters and the work God is doing in their lives where they are growing more and more in their faith.

In Romans 15:13 Paul identifies a key attribute of God as he writes, "May the God of hope".

When you think about who God is, and all the attributes associated with God, I think one of the often-overlooked ones is that He is the God of hope.

**If you are not very hopeful in some area of your life- bring that hopelessness to the God of hope and you will be filled with joy and peace (Romans 15:13).**

Jesus would say in Matthew 19:26, "but with God all things are possible." Jesus was clear that God is qualified as the God of hope.

Of course, the context of Jesus' profound statement is the story of the rich young man and Jesus is referring to salvation, but as you might know, sozo, the Greek word for salvation in verse Matthew 19:25 is bigger than everlasting life. Sozo means to save, keep safe and sound, to rescue from danger or destruction:

1. one (from injury or peril)

    1. to save a suffering one (from perishing), i.e. one suffering from disease, to make well, heal, restore to health

    2. to preserve one who is in danger of destruction, to save or rescue[4]

---

[4]https://www.blueletterbible.org/lang/lexicon/lexicon.cfm?Strongs=G4982&t=KJV

Because Jesus makes the statement "With man this is impossible, but with God all things are possible." The follow-up question is, "do we believe it"?  If you believe that with God all things are possible then you can have hope in all things and your peace will be protected. We will see this in a later chapter as this is reinforced in Philippians 4:7.

Some wake up in the morning and say, "Good Lord, it's morning" and there are those who wake up believing with God all things are possible and say, "Good Lord, it's morning." When we know of God as the great object of our hope that He is the God of hope it is a good morning Lord.

**Question #1 Where does hope come from?**

Romans 15:13 tells us the answer: "May the God of hope/(elpis)" Elpis in this instance means the author of hope. So, hope comes from God. He is the author of hope.

**The only source of true joy and peace is God Himself. The only way by which God can give any man joy and peace is by giving him Himself (Romans 15:13).**

At one time we were "without hope and without God," but "on Him we have set our hope" (Ephesians 2:12, 2 Corinthians 1:9-10).

Attach your hope to anything less than God and you set yourself up for failure and disappointment. But put your hope in Him and you'll reign in life with joy and peace.

I. The privileges of true Christians.
   1. Joy.
   2. Peace.
   3. Hope.

  II. The method of securing them.
   1. God the source.
   2. Faith in Christ the means.
   3. The Holy Ghost the agent

*(J. Lyth, D.D.)*[5]

## Question #2 How Do You Experience Joy and Peace? There is Only One Way: Trust in Him.

May the God of hope do something for you... fill you with all joy and peace. How?

[5] J.Lyth. Biblical Illustrator Volume 5.

As you trust in Him, so that you may overflow with hope by the power of the Holy Spirit.

God is willing and wanting to fill you with all joy and peace but He can't force it upon you, you have to trust Him as you believe in God's promises so that you may overflow with hope by the power of the Holy Spirit.

You might be thinking that there is a word that has been used that is a hope buster, "may".
I don't like the word may very much. I don't put much stock in it or trust it. We could make any outlandish statement we want and as long as we attach may to it, we are covered. "Pastor Matt Webster may one day win a Grammy for Best Male Pop Vocalist." For those of you that know me well, this is not ever going to happen. I have no vocal talent when it comes to singing, but if I used a "may" most people wouldn't challenge my statement.
May is often used as a who knows what the future might hold escape clause for any statement we might make. So, when we read Romans 15:13 it sounds like Paul is hedging his bet on God's response to your life.

"May the God of hope fill you with all joy and peace as you trust in Him, so that you may (or you may not) overflow with hope by the power of the Holy Spirit."

As we go to the Greek clarity springs forth because God is not selective here at all. God isn't saying some people will receive hope and peace will others might not. In the original Greek language, the word may is not found in the text at all. Instead, the word is (perisseuō): To make to abound, to be in abundance.

**It is not that you may or may not abound in hope, it is you will abound in abundance with hope and it is a work of the Holy Spirit (Romans 15:13).**

Before Paul would make this profound statement about God in Romans 15:13 that he is the "God of hope"- he first gave the greatest example of God delivering on something His people had hoped for the most, for the longest amount of time.
It was through God delivering on a centuries-upon-centuries old promise that the title "God of hope" becomes most appropriate.

What is the number one thing the Jews hoped for? A Messiah.

The God of hope came through when His people had all but given up hope. Now, Paul isn't writing this letter to the Jews but to the Gentile Romans. The twist is that these are the very same people the Jews were hoping the God of hope would send a Messiah to destroy. But the Messiah came to bring about salvation to all people, even the enemy of God's people, the Romans. Why? Because He is the God of hope for all people who would simply put their trust in Him.
So, Paul quotes the prophet Isaiah and it works beautifully because the last part is directed at the Romans.

Romans 15:12: "And again, Isaiah says, "The Root of Jesse will spring up," Paul quotes Isaiah 11:10 but does so using the Greek so the word changes from the Hebrew word (`amad) endure to (eimi) in the Greek: to happen, to exist. This shifts to the first person singular present indicative "I am". What Paul does is equate Jesus as being Divine. "I Am" is the name God gave of Himself to Moses.

"To lead": is one who will arise to rule over the lead nations;

Rule over is not a great translation, because who hopes in someone who rules over them?

The Greek word (archō) means to lead in Him the Gentiles (ethnos) will...

(elpizō) - to wait for salvation with joy and full confidence.

When you put all that Greek together the message is clear.
Romans 15:12 reads like this: The Root of Jesse (Jesus Christ) will happen to lead the nations (Jews and Gentiles) and in Him the Gentiles will hope or wait for salvation with joy and full confidence.

**Paul quotes the prophecy of Isaiah (11:10) as a reminder of what was most hoped for a (Savior/Messiah) that God delivered on the promise He made 750 years after He made the announcement.**

The answer to the promise was better than what the Jews imagined, it was salvation available to all people who believe.

What this means is that Romans 15:13 is our salvation story in a nutshell. Sure, we heard the Gospel in different ways at different times but the moment you and I first believed it was because of the author of hope. The author of hope poured into our lives, abundant peace and joy as we first believed in Jesus. This was a result of the Holy Spirit who filled our hearts and for the first time, we expected good and were confident of everlasting life.

When you have bad news and your peace is threatened, how can you expect good? Trust in God.

I used to meet with other pastors regularly many years ago. At one meeting we were discussing how difficult Monday mornings can be.

One pastor shared how his past Sunday service was incredible. People were crying tears of joy, there was such a feeling of peace as He has shared his heart about VBS and the difference the Gospel makes in a child's life. After everyone left the room the pastor walked to the back of the Sanctuary and the VBS sign-up list had only one name on it, his wife. He told us how that moment had left him discouraged. Another pastor asked, "what do you do when things like that happen in life"?

Moments like that can be discouraging, not hopeful. You can look at that sign-up sheet over and over and the names will not magically appear. Your situation might not change or get any better.

The good news is there is an answer to the pastor's question. There is an answer to our hopeless, depressing situations and that answer is found in Romans 15.

God is the author of hope. Trust in Him. If you are short on volunteers for VBS, take it to God, trust that He will provide what you need and wisdom in what to do. I know from experience as the Holy Spirit sets my spiritual eyes on Jesus, I am filled beyond the brim with a sense of joy, peace, and abounding hope even when situations remained the same. A situation may not change, but the way I see my situation does. He always gives me what I need for the things He is calling me too. He is my provider. He is my hope. If no one volunteers for VBS are you alright if you don't try to force it to happen? What else might God be leading you to do instead?

I love what comes after is a sub-header that was inserted later, "Paul the Minister to the Gentiles".

While others in the early beginnings of the church had trouble accepting the Gentiles, Paul moves forward in his calling to them because Paul was revealing the true nature of God our Father- that He is the God of hope. God would take a zealous Jew who killed Christians and in Christ radically changes his life to become the minister of the Gospel of grace to the Gentiles. That is God doing the impossible once again. He truly is the God of hope.

So, whatever you might be discouraged about, God right now through the Holy Spirit is leading you to bring your discouragement to Him because He desires to fill your life with joy and peace and give you hope.

# Chapter 2 Peace With God

In chapter 1 we began with a very general definition for peace. This first definition we labeled as facet number one is: security, safety, and prosperity.

This definition of peace is felt by both believers and unbelievers alike and can vary at moments in a person's life. No matter how great a person's level of security, safety, and prosperity is during their lives on earth none of that will matter if they don't possess the second facet of peace that deals with eternal life.

Peace Facet #2 (eirēnē):
of Christianity, the tranquil state of a soul assured of its salvation through Christ, and so fearing nothing from God and content with its earthly lot, of whatsoever sort that is

This second facet of peace is a gift of grace given to all who receive the Savior's sacrifice on their behalf for sin. What this means is this second facet of peace, "peace with God, is something a believer will always have, unlike the first facet of peace that can come and go.

At the cross, and before you did a single thing, you received peace with God and complete forgiveness (2 Corinthians 5:19, Colossians 2:13).

When you were placed in Jesus, you gained His acceptance (Ephesians 1:6), His righteousness (Romans 1:17), His holiness (1 Corinthians 1:3), and His eternal perfection (Hebrews 10:4). Because of what we have been given through the finished work of Jesus, we are assured of salvation through Christ. We fear no judgment or wrath to us from God, since our sin is removed there is nothing left to judge. Peace with God leads forth contentment in our lives, whatever may come.

Peter would write, "may grace and peace be multiplied unto you" and we learned that the way this happens is found in his writing 2 Peter 1:2: "Grace and peace be yours in abundance through the knowledge of God and of Jesus our Lord."

We can receive the salvation of the Lord for the things that come against us on earth.

Whatever does happen we can also find contentment in all things as Paul did in prison as he wrote, "I am not saying this because I am in need, for I have learned to be content whatever the circumstances. I know what it is to be in need, and I know what it is to have plenty. I have learned the secret of being content in any and every situation, whether well fed or hungry, whether living in plenty or in want. I can do all this through him who gives me strength" (Philippians 4:11-13).

Paul found that God equips us with strength for the things we face, so there is no need to become discontent. Ultimately, even if Paul were to die, the promise is of everlasting life, and so peace could be found even in the most painful circumstances of our lives.

"but will have sufficient courage so that now as always Christ will be exalted in my body, whether by life or by death. For to me, to live is Christ and to die is gain" (Philippians 1:20b-21).

The cross is the symbol of our victory and peace with God.

Within that second facet/definition of peace, we discover our spiritual state **before we received salvation through Christ, we were not at peace with God because sin separated us from a holy and righteous God.**

Romans in 5:1 is the key text of our understanding of how peace with God is received.

"Therefore, since we have been justified through faith, we have peace with God through our Lord Jesus Christ" (Romans 5:1).

The first word in Romans 5:1 is "therefore" which gives us the clue that Paul is mid-thought when he comes to this remarkable statement about how we have and hold peace with God. Paul did not intend Romans 5:1 to be separated from his main idea in Romans 4. Our peace with God and our understanding of it, further insight is gained as we explore chapter four.

Romans 4:3: "Abraham believed God, and it was credited to him as righteousness."

Righteousness or right standing with God was based upon faith for Abraham, not law living as this is reinforced in verse thirteen.

Romans 4:13-15: "It was not through the law that Abraham and his offspring received the promise that he would be heir of the world, but through the righteousness that comes by faith. For if those who depend on the law are heirs, faith means nothing and the promise is worthless, because the law brings wrath."

**The point that Paul is making is that peace with God does not come from law-based living. Peace with God is a free gift that comes through faith by God's grace (Romans 4:13-15a).**

Law-based living will not ever result in peace in your life! Peace with God cannot be earned, it comes only through faith in Jesus.

Romans 4:16: "Therefore, the promise comes by faith, so that it may be by grace and may be guaranteed to all Abraham's offspring—not only to those who are of the law but also to those who have the faith of Abraham. He is the father of us all."

Now we can carry the main thought of Romans chapter four into Romans 5:1.

"Therefore, since we have been justified through faith, "we have" Greek word (echo) [to have and to hold]. No one and nothing can take from us peace with God.

Now peace with God is extraordinary because knowing that our salvation is secure in Christ gives us this form of peace: the tranquil state of a soul assured of its salvation through Christ, and so fearing nothing from God and content with its earthly lot, of whatsoever sort that is.

Having this extraordinary peace with God also leads to something happening in our lives as a result (boasting in something).

"through whom we have gained access by faith into this grace in which we now stand. And we boast in the hope of the glory of God" (Romans 5:2).

Do you know that you have been put or made firm and established in the grace of our Lord Jesus Christ?

"We boast in the hope in the glory of God." Doxa (glory) in the context it is written means we boast that we belong to Jesus and that is our hope.

There is a very wealthy Hollywood celebrity who adopted a child and raised the child with all the opportunity in the world to succeed and flourish and enjoy life living with such a prestigious family name. However, instead of walking in who they are, as the child grew into adulthood, she squandered the opportunity before her making one big mistake after another. I read an interview where the adopted child said, "I don't want anything to do with the family name, I'll carve my own path." An outsider can see where the path apart from her father would lead. Her life was a lot like a modern-day version of the prodigal son. Hopefully, she will come to her senses too before it is too late.

Paul writes that faith in Jesus led to peace with God and also put us in and established us firmly in His grace.

Our response should be rejoicing or boasting in our family name, that we belong to Jesus. We can choose to walk forward into our future with great hope of what God will do in our life simply because we are His child and He dearly loves us.

I was a pastor for several years before I knew what I had access to during hospital visitations.

There is a hospital somewhere in Michigan that has a secret wall. It is near the elevators and when you press on the wall and do the truffle shuffle the wall will open where you will find a secret set of elevators so you don't have to wait and stop and each level. What a great invention for medical professionals, clergy, and anyone who at times may need to get to a certain hospital room in a hurry.

I didn't know I was allowed to use the secret elevator. I didn't even know they existed until after I received my badge. As Christians, we have so much available to us being set in God's grace. Let's tap into it. Let's take the secret spiritual elevators to the throne of grace (Hebrews 4:16). "Therefore, since we have been justified through faith, we have peace with God through our Lord Jesus Christ." Jesus gave us our badge of peace with God, why wouldn't we want to go to the throne of grace, and go often? It is not a surprise that what you will find at the throne since you have peace with God, is "mercy and grace to help in time of need."

Another insight I gained from Romans 5:2 is that **we have hope despite what we see, despite what we feel because we have been justified by faith and we have and hold the very peace of God through our Lord Jesus Christ (Romans 5:1)**.

There is more to our relationship with God because of our connection to Christ. In the Greek, it says we are acceptable to God and have the assurance of God's favorable disposition towards us.

Have you ever had a boss or a teacher that just seemed to favor you? You'd get the employee of the month award all the time. You didn't have to wonder how the boss felt or your favorite teacher felt about you because their actions showed you were valued and appreciated. God is always favorably disposed towards us. When bad things happen, you have the God of the Universe who is for you (Romans 8:31). Your gained access (faith belief) that Jesus is the Messiah, has led you <u>into this grace in which we now stand.</u>

(histēmi)- to stand immovable, stand firm, continue safe and sound, stand unharmed, to stand ready or prepared, to be of a steadfast mind- in our firm foundation who is Jesus.

<u>And we boast in the hope of the glory of God.</u> We boast or we rejoice in (elpis) an expectation of good, joyful and confident expectation of eternal salvation, the thing hoped for.

So, we don't need to ask God to give us hope; instead, ask Him to reveal His love. He will! He has! To know His love is to know that your Father can be trusted. He has promised to take care of you, to watch over you, to supply all your needs, so expect good things from Him.

Brennan Manning wrote in *The Ragamuffin Gospel*:

"Abba is not our enemy. If we think that, we are wrong. Abba is not intent on trying and tempting and testing us. If we think that, we are wrong. Abba does not prefer and promote suffering and pain. If we think that, we are wrong. Jesus brings good news about the father, not bad news. We need a new kind of relationship with the Father that drives out fear and mistrust and anxiety and guilt, that permits us to be hopeful and joyous, trusting and compassionate. We have to be converted from the bad news to the good news, from expecting nothing to expecting something." (p.76)[6]


To understand that God's favor goes with you and is over your life is illustrated in this Old Testament passage.


Judges 18:5-6: "Then they said to him, "Please inquire of God to learn whether our journey will be successful.

---

[6] Brennan Manning. The Ragamuffin Gospel. Multnomah. 76.

The priest answered them, "Go in peace. Your journey has the Lord's approval."

If I could guarantee a most prosperous year but you had to first experience some really difficult challenges, would you agree to that? I know I would because through the tough times I have hope for great success that I am being moved toward. When we know the outcome is a success, living the story becomes quite exhilarating (Judges 18:5-6).

"The priest answered them, "Go in peace" (Shalom): completeness, soundness, welfare, peace with God especially in covenant relationship.

The people of God wanted to know, "is our journey going to be successful?" Wouldn't you like to know if your journey will be successful? We all want to know just like the Danites, is God in this endeavor, will my journey be a successful one?

In your life journey, go in peace (shalom)- completeness soundness, welfare because you know God is in a covenant relationship with you. Go in complete peace because Jesus had died to give you His peace with God.

Under the New Covenant, we are given the opportunity to receive salvation as a free gift (Ephesians 2:8-9). Our responsibility is to exercise faith in Christ (throughout our journey) and know that our journey will be a success and that our journey is one of purpose.

Remember Philippians 1:6 being confident of this (being confident the journey ahead will be a success) because He who began a good work in you will carry it on to completion until the day of Christ Jesus.

The Danites needed to know if their journey would be a success because the covenant at that time was between them and God. If they did something wrong, their journey would be a failure. Since Jesus is our success and satisfied the demands of the Law we go forth in victory. Through the life-giving Holy Spirit who lives in all believers (Romans 8:9-11), we share in the inheritance of Christ and enjoy a permanent, unbroken relationship with God (Hebrews 9:15).

Deuteronomy 28:1 "If you fully obey the Lord your God and carefully follow all his commands I give you today, the Lord your God will set you high above all the nations on earth. All these blessings will come on you and accompany you if you obey the Lord your God: You will be blessed when you come in and blessed when you go out (Deuteronomy 28:1-2,6)"

So, when you read the qualifications for the blessing (Deuteronomy 28:1-2) and you look to yourself, you will realize you are unqualified (in and of yourself for them). They had to "inquire of God whether their journey will be successful" (Judges 18:5).

This also means based upon God's people worshiping false gods at the end of Judges 18, blessings are not coming, but curses instead. Deuteronomy 28:15: "However, if you do not obey the Lord your God and do not carefully follow all His commands and decrees I am giving you today, all these curses will come on you and overtake you".

Here is the good news, in New Covenant Living, Jesus is your qualification for God's blessings. Jesus already came to fulfill the Law (Matthew 5:17), you just need to cash in on the blessings that are yours in Christ by faith.

Jesus redeemed us from the curse of the law (Galatians 3:13). If the curse of the law is gone, then what is left? The blessings are left for us in Jesus.

It is no longer a question of how much or how well you have kept God's commandments. It is a question of how much you can believe God for His blessings. We like the Danites, received God's Word, as God send His Son who is the Word, and became flesh so that we might have peace with God through Him. So, by faith, go in shalom: completeness, soundness, welfare, peace because we are restored in relationship with God in a covenant relationship that is not based upon our ability to uphold it.

There is one more thing to know, just like the Danites, we still need to go forward and battle the forces of darkness, believing in the report or the Word of the Lord.

The Bible says (Joshua 1:8) that you will make your way prosperous when you (hagah) speak God's Word. So, speak forth God's Word (Jesus Christ) who is our victory over the areas in which you want to see breakthroughs and you will have success.

Confessing God's Word does not move God to do things for you. It is not a formula. God already moved when He gave Jesus to die for you. However, as you confess His Word, it moves you from a position of doubt to faith. It moves your heart from a position of "Is it true?" to "I believe it!" When that happens, your way is prosperous and you will have success.

# Chapter 3
# Peace of Christ

I could always use some more peace in my life. So, let's recap the peace facets we have discovered up until this chapter. In chapter 1 we examined a common greeting Paul used, "peace be with you". In this case, the way Paul used it, illustrated the fact that peace can come and go and vary at certain points in our lives. In chapter 2 we focused on peace with God which is another aspect of the Greek definition for peace (eirēnē). The difference between the two is that our relationship with God (salvation) does not change, but the peace we receive can waver.

In the third facet of peace, we will discover that this peace is something we always have, but we may or may not allow it to rule our hearts. Peace facet number three is unique in that it is the kind of peace we always have like, "peace with God" however, we experience it more like "peace be with you".

Colossians 3:15 says, "Let the peace of Christ rule in your hearts, since as members of one body you were called to peace. And be thankful."

This verse makes me laugh because Paul tells us "to let the peace of Christ rule in our hearts" and then he ends with "and be thankful". I have never seen someone who has the peace of Christ ruling in their hearts be ungrateful. It seems redundant to add the and be thankful part, but there is a reason for it.

"Let the peace (eirēnē) of Christ"

Peace Facet #3 (eirēnē)

 of the Messiah's peace

the way that leads to peace (salvation)

Did you know that peace is a blessing from the Lord? The Psalmist wrote (29:11) "The LORD gives strength to His people; the LORD blesses his people with peace."

You are a child of God which makes you one of God's people and the promise is He will give you strength and He will give you peace.

Question: How did God give us peace?
Answer: Through Jesus.

John 16:33: "I have told you these things, so that in me you may have peace. In this world you will have trouble. But take heart! I have overcome the world."

John 14:27 "Peace I leave with you; my peace I give you. I do not give to you as the world gives. Do not let your hearts be troubled and do not be afraid."

I love that the peace Jesus gives, He will never take back. He doesn't give like the world where our gifts might be taken back from us. Jesus isn't going to take back His peace, His peace is there for you always. What that means is we are the ones who get to decide on whether or not we will let the peace Christ gives, rule in our hearts.

You might have noticed that within peace facet #3 a word is added in parenthesis (salvation).

I am grateful for the addition of the word salvation. The Greek word for salvation is sozo:

to save, keep safe and sound, to rescue from danger or destruction

    a. one (from injury or peril)

1. to save a suffering one (from perishing), i.e. one suffering from disease, to make well, heal, restore to health

2. to preserve one who is in danger of destruction, to save or rescue[7]

**Let the peace of Christ, as in the salvation of the Lord,** (that He saves us, keeps us safe and sound, rescues us from danger or destruction, heals us from disease, makes us well and restores us to health) **lead you to His peace ruling in your hearts.**

This is a little bit similar to chapter one in that the decision is yours to make. You could at any time allow the peace of Christ to rule in your heart or not.

Rule (brabeuō): to decide, determine to direct, control, rule, to be an umpire.

You are the umpire. Life throws you a curveball and you decide and make the judgment call about it. Let's choose the peace of Christ. When the pitch comes and it looks bad, the Lord will keep me safe

---

[7] https://www.biblestudytools.com/lexicons/greek/nas/sozo.html

and sound, rescue and restore me and He will make me well.

How can you say that with any certainty when people sometimes die? This is where you need to have an eternal perspective like Paul did when he writes Timothy.

2 Timothy 4:17-18: "But the Lord stood by me and strengthened me, so that through me the message would be fully proclaimed, and all the Gentiles would hear it. So I was delivered from the mouth of the lion. And the Lord will rescue me from every evil action and bring me safely into His heavenly kingdom. To Him be the glory forever and ever. Amen."

Paul was killed for his faith, yet he wasn't wrong about the Lord bringing Him safe into His heavenly kingdom. Paul successfully finished his course on earth and God fulfilled His end of the covenant, bringing Paul safely to heaven. Do you believe a loved one who was sick on earth will be sick in heaven? Or will God bring them safely, healed, restored, totally well into His heavenly Kingdom where there is no sickness no sadness and no suffering?

No matter what comes, you get to be the umpire and decide to let the peace of Christ rule in your heart.

Now in Colossians 3:15: "...you were called to peace." is not written in the original Greek manuscript. It reads like this:

"Let the peace of Christ rule in your hearts to which indeed you were called in one body and be thankful."

Rereading it in the Greek brings clarity. Paul is talking about our interactions with other believers. **You have a calling to the Body of Christ (Colossians 3:15).** We are to use our spiritual gifting for works of ministry to build up the body (Ephesians 4:12) that is our calling.

This gets me excited because I wonder what amazing gifts and talents you might have to bring glory to God that I might get to enjoy. I also dream about how God might use the spiritual gifts He has given me to bless you. Together what a masterpiece work of God we all are together as the body.

We see what Paul is writing here is the church universal. A brother or sister in Christ doesn't have to belong to Acts 433 Church for me to be blessed by their works of ministry. Just as the majority of the people who will read this book won't belong to Acts 433 and hopefully will be blessed by this work as well.

All of this leads to thanksgiving.

So when I correctly read Colossians 3:15 "Let the peace of Christ rule in your hearts to which indeed you were called in one body and be thankful." The thankful part is no longer out of place or redundant. I am giving thanks for my calling in the body and I am giving thanks for your calling and activity in the body, all the while choosing the peace of Christ to rule in my heart. And we partake in thankfulness (eucharistos) mindful of the fact that we are well-favored by God.

The next two verses are essential to answer the question, "How do I let the peace of Christ rule in my heart"?

Colossians 3:16,17:

"Let the message of Christ dwell among you richly as you teach and admonish one another with all wisdom through psalms, hymns, and songs from the Spirit, singing to God with gratitude in your hearts. And whatever you do, whether in word or deed, do it all in the name of the Lord Jesus, giving thanks to God the Father through him."

What I see in this text are:

## <u>5 Ways to Let the Peace of Christ Rule Your Heart</u>

1) "Dwell in the Message of Christ Richly"

This is a reinforcement of how we multiple peace facet number 1 in our lives. God's Word tells us that when you receive revelation in the knowledge of Jesus, it will cause grace and peace to be multiplied in your life. It will cause you to receive all things that pertain to life and godliness (2 Peter 1:3).

In Isaiah 26:3, it says "You will keep in perfect peace those whose minds are steadfast, because they trust in you." As our trust is in Jesus there is perfect peace to be found.

I remember going to Detroit Tigers baseball games as a young child. When you are young, the first several trips to downtown Detroit are eye-opening. I am not sure that I even blinked the entire time I was there. There was so much to take in. The sights, the smells, the buildings, and the busyness in the streets. People coming and going, people selling peanuts, parking attendants waving flags, ticket scalpers shouting out to everyone who passed, "I've got four tickets here, real good seats". It was exciting and overwhelming all at the same time. If I had to make my way to the game all by myself without a parent to guide me, there would be no peace to be found in my life. However, because I know my parents, I can trust they will lead me safely to my seats and though a lot is going on around me, I have peace within me and I believe the trip to the destination will be rather exciting.

The word dwell used in Colossians 3:15 is a Greek metaphor meaning to dwell in one and influence one for good. And the word richly can be translated as abundantly- so I take this to mean that as the message of Christ fills our lives- we dwell in it and it influences us to the abundance of spiritual blessings that are ours in Christ and the peace of Christ reigns in us.

2) "Admonish on Another with Wisdom from the Spirit"

One of the things that can make my day, week, month, or even my year is when there is an opportunity to minister to someone who is struggling with something that is happening to them or to someone they love. Whether they are faced with having to make some important life decisions, or simply not knowing what to do in their current situation, the Holy Spirit will give me some insight at the moment with a verse or word for them. As a result of the revelation in the knowledge of Jesus, it will cause grace and peace to be multiplied in that person's life and then because I was a part of that focused time dwelling richly in the message of Christ, grace and peace are multiplied in my life too.

3) "Sing to God with Gratitude in Your Hearts"

"Nobody knows the trouble I've seen." If we stopped the song right there, that would be the most depressing song of all time.  But let's allow the song to continue,

"Nobody knows but He knows my sorrow
Yes, nobody knows the trouble I've seen
But glory, Hallelujah"[8]

As a church sometimes we got stuck on the first line and the song emanating from our lives is a blues song.

One of my favorite movies is *Adventures in Babysitting*. There is a line in that movie

---

[8] Louis Armstrong. Nobody Knows The Trouble I've Seen. 1962.

from B.B. King, "No one leaves without singing the Blues." I wish the church had a similar attitude, "nobody leaves without singing to God with gratitude in their hearts." You can't force gratitude, but my desire is for all believers to have the peace of Christ ruling in their hearts and this happens as we forget the blues, and we sing to God with gratitude in our hearts. He knows our pain.

Hebrews 4:15: "For we do not have a high priest who is unable to empathize with our weaknesses, but we have one who has been tempted in every way, just as we are--yet he did not sin."

"Nobody knows but He knows my sorrow."

4) "Do All in the Name of the Lord"

If we could look at all the things we do as we do them in the name of the Lord that would change the perspective we have on mundane tasks.

Do you know what tries to rob me of my joy? A sink that is full of dishes. I didn't know a family of five was capable of using so many dishes in one day until I had three kids. The dishwasher has different cycles you can choose so when we first got ours I had it set on the ultimate cycle which takes over four hours. The problem is I don't have four hours to run a cycle, the dirty dishes will take over. I need a turbo setting. Just thinking about dishes gets me worked up and not feeling very peaceful. The shift in my perspective comes when I can view dishwashing as something I can do in the name of the Lord. I tell my echo dot to play Hillsong worship and now I turn the chore into an opportunity to let the peace of Christ rule in my heart.

5) "Give Thanks to God through Jesus"

At this point I am still doing the dishes in the name of the Lord, it takes me so long that it carried from point four into point five. As Alexa plays Hillsong Radio I am singing (not very well but joyfully to God) with gratitude in my heart for many things. Thank you that you provided food for my family to make these dishes dirty. The peace of Christ is ruling in my heart as I clean the dishes and it is a miracle to behold. Ultimately, I see the provisions God has made for me in Jesus and I give thanks to God through Christ.

seek
PEACE
+ pursue it
PSALM 34:14

So far, we have looked at many different facets of peace and answered some important questions such as:

- Peace be with You (What is Peace? How do we have it multiplied unto us?)
- Peace with God (How are we given peace with God? Is this a permanent state we are in with Him?)
- Peace of Christ (Will Jesus ever take back the gift of His peace? When trouble comes how does the peace of Christ ruling in our hearts help us?)

After we understand the peace of Christ given to us and the peace we have with God, it is important to understand why we must now seek peace. If we already have peace, why should we then have to seek or pursue it like the Psalmist and the writer of Hebrews says? In a perfect world (heaven) we won't, but we live in a fallen world that has been marred by sin and inhabited by both children of light and children of darkness (1 Thessalonians 5:5).

Some people do not know the Lord's peace and there are others who have it but don't live in it, so it is very easy to not be at peace with someone else whether that is a believer or non-believer.

Did you know that before the fall of man there was peace in the world? The Bible offers a glimpse of how restoration in Jesus' kingdom will once again restore peace.

Isaiah 65:25: "The wolf and the lamb shall feed together, and the lion shall eat straw like the bullock: and dust shall be the serpent's meat. They shall not hurt nor destroy in all my holy mountain, saith the LORD."

There will be a full restoration of Eden that was lost with sin (Revelation 22). And it appears that in Isaiah there is an implied comparison between Adam and Christ. We know that all the afflictions of the present life flowed from the sin of Adam; for at that time we were deprived of the dominion and sovereignty which God had given to man over animals of every kind (Genesis 1:28).

Before sin, animals bowed cheerfully to the dominion of man and were obedient to his will; but now animals rise against man, and even war against their own kind. Adam's disobedience overthrew God's established order of things. But Christ will bring back everything to its condition and rightful order.

"And the lion shall eat straw like the ox." The lion shall no longer seek his prey. This is a picture of how life in the Garden of Eden will be.

In the eleventh chapter of Isaiah, we are taught the nature of men before the Lord receive them into His fold as being cruel and untamed beasts. Only when the Lord subdues their wicked inclination will they abstain from their furious desire to harm.

Permanent peace is coming again with Jesus as it did with His birth. **Peace on earth was the baby Jesus himself on earth (Micah 5:5).** Micah 5:5 prophecies: this One (the Messiah) will be our peace. In Luke 2:14: "The angels said peace on earth to those on whom His favor rests."

Permanent favor of God forever is for those who are in Jesus (Luke 2:14) because we are given His peace, His standing with God. God's favor and Jesus the Savior are synonymous. Peace comes with Christ and so those who have His peace should be the ones who pursue peace with all men.

On the night of His birth, we get a mighty shout. "Peace has come to earth!" As Mary discovered and we're still learning, we are highly favored by God. Because the Lord is with us. You cannot have the Lord and be anything other than highly favored. He is a magnet to His favor. That is why Immanuel is such an amazing declaration. I am highly favored by God that He would remain with me always and forever.

Peace on earth came through Jesus at His birth. His presence brought peace to the earth and His return will establish peace forever in His kingdom. "The wolf and the lamb shall feed together, and the lion shall eat straw like the bullock: and dust shall be the serpent's meat. They shall not hurt nor destroy in all my holy mountain, saith the LORD."

Hebrews 12:14: NASB: "Pursue peace with all men, and the sanctification without which no one will see the Lord."

There is no doubt, as you study Hebrews you will see how educated the writer of Hebrews is in the Old Testament. Hebrews 12:14 most have been influenced by Psalm 34:14: "Turn from evil and do good; seek peace and pursue it."

"Pursue (diōkō): seek after eagerly, pursue peace with all men".

It is clear that if you want to have peace with others you will have to seek eagerly after it.

There is a famous hymn that goes:

"Let there be peace on earth
And let it begin with me
Let There Be Peace on Earth
The peace that was meant to be
With God as our Father
Brothers all are we
Let me walk with my brother
In perfect harmony."[9]

---

[9] Jill Jackson-Miller and Sy Miller
https://en.wikipedia.org/wiki/Let_There_Be_Peace_on_Earth_(song) 1955.

Our hearts ruling with the peace of Christ
will have the desire to have peace with all
men.

There is a second instruction in Hebrews
12:14 as well- "And the sanctification"

The question that comes is, "what does
sanctification have to do with pursuing
peace with all men?"

Before we can answer that question, we
need to ask another: "What is
sanctification?"

(Hagiasmos)- the state of purity, holiness.
An advanced definition comes from the
root of the word sanctify which means to
set apart to God for His use.

Paul Ellis writing about the holiness of God
said, "To worship God in the beauty of his
holiness is to be awestruck by the infinite
sweep and scale of his sublimity. It is to
become lost in the limitless landscape of
His loveliness. Holiness is not one aspect
of God's character; it is the whole package
in glorious unity. It is the adjective that
precedes all other attributes."[10]

---

[10] https://escapetoreality.org/2020/01/23/the-whole-meaning-of-holiness/

So now that we have a definition of sanctification what does sanctification have to do with pursuing peace with all men?
"Pursue peace with all men, and the sanctification without which no one will see the Lord."

"To see God is a Hebrew phrase meaning to enjoy Him."[11] We enjoy God because Christ has purified us and made us whole. We are set apart to be used by God because we are in Christ. Because of our positional holiness as being found in Christ, it is now possible to eagerly pursue behavioral holiness which takes us to our fourth facet/definition of peace that is referenced in Hebrews 12:14.

Peace Facet #4 (eirēnē)
a state of national tranquillity
1) exemption from the rage and havoc of war
2) peace between individuals, i.e. harmony, concord

Technically speaking, these are two separate definitions of peace that I listed. One is talking about peace between

---

[11] Adam Clarke Commentary
https://www.studylight.org/commentary/hebrews/12-14.html

nations and the other is peace between individuals. However, both definitions still fall under the framework of "peace with all men."

Wrapped up in our exhortation "to be holy" (1 Peter 1:15) is our calling to live in our Christ-given identity and in so doing we will experience the enjoyment of time spent with God, (Hebrews 12:14).

"Without holiness no one will see the Lord," is not a threat but a promise of what transpires because we are holy we will see the Lord and we will enjoy His presence with us now.

Question: How do I eagerly pursue peace with someone who is not bent on peace toward me?

Answer: Peter addresses this in 1 Peter 3:8-22. It is a rather lengthy passage so if you would like to better understand verse 15 and how that works you can find the explanation illustrated in Church Membership: God's Good Purpose Fulfilled in You.[12]

---

[12] Rev. Dr. Matthew Webster. Church Membership: God's Good Purposed Fulfilled in You. (47-50).

"Finally, all of you, be like-minded, be sympathetic, love one another, be compassionate and humble. Do not repay evil with evil or insult with insult.

On the contrary, repay evil with blessing, because to this you were called so that you may inherit a blessing. For, "Whoever would love life and see good days must keep their tongue from evil and their lips from deceitful speech. They must turn from evil and do good; they must seek peace and pursue it. For the eyes of the Lord are on the righteous and his ears are attentive to their prayer, but the face of the Lord is against those who do evil." Who is going to harm you if you are eager to do good? But even if you should suffer for what is right, you are blessed. "Do not fear their threats; do not be frightened" (1 Peter 3:8-14).

Enduring unjust suffering and doing it patiently shows the world, God. It makes the suffering of Christ real to people. It makes peace possible when others are bent on harm and destruction. People can see that this is the way Jesus was. And if you have seen Jesus, you have seen the Father (John 14:9). So, this kind of demeanor shows God by showing Christ his Son.

When you endure unjust suffering, you are not saying justice doesn't matter; what you are saying is that God is the final judge and will settle accounts justly.
So, this is our calling to suffer unjustly (1 Peter 2:21), not to hurt back those who hurt us (1 Peter 2:23), and this is not a rule to keep but a miracle to be experienced, it's a grace to be received (1 Peter 2:20).

1 Peter 3:9, "Do not repay evil for evil or reviling for reviling, but on the contrary, bless, for to this you were called, that you may obtain a blessing." There is a great blessing in (forgiveness) Peter says and part of that blessing is that your bitterness and anger are removed and the pain will be taken too. Peace with all men comes by way of not repaying evil for evil.

Pursuing peace with all men is what peacemakers do.

"Blessed are the peacemakers, for they will be called children of God" (Matthew 5:9).

Blessed (makarios): supremely blessed, fortunate, well-off, happy.

**A defining characteristic of peacemakers is that they are supremely blessed, fortunate and happy.**

Who are the peacemakers? We are given the answer in the last part of the same verse "they will be called children of God".

1 John 3:1-2a: "The Father has loved us so much that we are called children of God. And we really are his children. The reason the people in the world do not know us is that they have not known him. Dear friends, now we are children of God..."

Question: So who are the peacemakers? Answer: Children of God.

Believers are the peacemakers because they are the ones who have the very peace of Christ. But why is it that sometimes Christians don't seem to be very peaceful? The answer is from our last chapter, each child of God gets to decide on whether or not to let the peace of Christ rule in their hearts (Colossians 3:15).

Being a peacemaker is what Jesus can do in our lives. That's why Jesus said, "I am the vine; you are the branches. If you remain in me and I in you, you will bear much fruit; apart from me you can do nothing" (John 15:5).

Do you see yourself in Christ as a peacemaker? Do you see yourself as one who is supremely blessed because you are a child of God? If so, you are equipped to pursue peace with all men.

Peace is worth more than all worldly possessions; in addition, God rewards it even in this life.
St. Vincent de Paul

Depending on which translation of the Bible you read the number of times the word peace is used can vary wildly. In the King James Version, peace is used 429 times, but in the New International Version, it is only used 252 times.

Whenever peace does not appear, a similar word such as safety, silence, quiet rest, still, contentment, satisfy, ease, etc... is used instead. If you are reading some of the verses I listed and another word other than peace is present, those other words are acceptable usages of the Greek word (eirēnē) and the Hebrew word (shalom).

It is remarkable how amazing the peace we have been given is. To conclude our study together some rewards are given to us for having peace. St. Vincent de Paul said, "Peace is worth more than all worldly possessions; in addition, God rewards it even in this life."

Peace truly is a beautiful gift that Jesus has given to all believers.

The rewards of peace magnify the truth that God is so good to produce peace in us and then reward us for it. All fruit we bear in our lives comes from abiding in Jesus (John 15) and we will be rewarded for the fruits that Jesus helps us to bear (Romans 2:6-7, Revelation 22:12).

Within the definition of peace, we already discovered a plethora of rewards. The reward of salvation, safety, security, prosperity, and a tranquil state of our soul. However, the Bible lists other rewards as well and that is what we will focus on in this chapter.

James 3:18 says, "Peacemakers who sow in peace reap a harvest of righteousness.

**#1st Reward of Peace: Peacemakers reap a harvest of righteousness (Peacemakers will show the way to receive Jesus' peace).**

This would also be reflected in the storing up of treasures in heaven (Matthew 6:20).

What we learned from the previous chapter is who the peacemakers are.

Matthew 5:9: "Blessed are the peacemakers, for they will be called children of God.
When we break down James 3:18 in the Greek this truth is amplified and it incredible to see.

The previous translation isn't incorrect but a better translation should read as such: "And the seed whose fruit is righteousness is sown in peace by those who make peace."

The Greek word "the seed whose fruit is" (karpos)- is defined as the fruit of the trees, vines, of the fields. This is connecting us to Christ's righteousness. Our connection to Him makes us righteous. He is our righteousness.

**Christ the Righteous One who gave us His righteousness, in us will sow or spread peace out of our lives. This will lead others to the way of Messiah's peace (which is salvation).**

**#2nd Reward of Peace: Joy.**

Proverbs 12:20: "Deceit is in the hearts of those who plot evil, but those who promote peace have joy."

We have a comparison and contrast going on in Proverbs. Those who plot evil have deceit in their hearts.
Think of any Indiana Jones or James Bond villain that was ever created. What they all have in common would be evil plots, deceit in their hearts, and an absence of peace. Their rule is characterized by force and fear, there is no peace to be found in the realm they control.

As you look at the context surrounding Proverbs 12:20 all of Proverbs 12 is a back and forth comparison of evil, wicked, foolish people, versus the righteous, honest, noble, wise, children of God. One of the verses that stands out to me is Proverbs 12:2: "Good people obtain favor from the LORD, but he condemns those who devise wicked schemes."

No one is "good" apart from Jesus. In Jesus, He has made us saints the very definition of a good person. For saints, there is obtained favor which leads to peace. This is the tie in from verse two to verse twelve.

"Those who promote" (ya`ats): counselors or consultants of peace (shalom): completeness, soundness, welfare, peace, health, prosperity, quiet, contentment [this can only be found for those who are in a covenantal relationship with God] have joy.

Proverbs 12 is incredible to view as a picture that portrays the life of a person found in Christ. Here is what is said about the righteous children of God from the first verse until the fourteenth:

- Loves discipline loves knowledge (verse 1)
- Favor from the Lord (verse 2)
- Cannot be uprooted (verse 3)
- Their plans are just (verse 5)
- Their speech rescues (verse 6)
- Their house stands firm (verse 7)
- Praised according to their prudence (verse 8)
- Care for the needs of their animals (verse 10)
- Their employees are blessed (verse 11)
- They endure (verse 12)
- Innocent escape trouble (verse 13)
- Fruit of their lips, people are filled with good things (verse 14)

- Work of their hands brings rewards (verse 14)

What a beautiful portrait of the life of the righteous and how their lives will have peace.

Philippians 4:6-7: "Do not be anxious about anything, but in every situation, by prayer and petition, with thanksgiving, present your requests to God. And the peace of God, which transcends all understanding, will guard your hearts and your minds in Christ Jesus."

We have peace with God and so Philippians 4:6-7 reveals some of those rewards. Paul says in Philippians 4:7 that "the peace of God transcends all understanding."

## #3rd **Reward of Peace: transcends all understanding.**

Why is this a reward to have our understanding transcended?

I can tell you from experience that when I have encountered difficult moments, fearful moments, the one thing that does not seem to be present as those events come upon me suddenly is a sense of peace. However, in this verse, we find that our thoughts can be surpassed with the mind of Christ that we have (1 Corinthians 2:16).

Transcends (hyperechō): to excel, to be superior, better than, to surpass Understanding (nous) the mind, comprising alike the faculties of perceiving and understanding and those of feeling, judging, determining - (the capacity for spiritual truth).

God said through the prophet Isaiah, "For my thoughts are not your thoughts, neither are your ways my ways," declares the LORD. "As the heavens are higher than the earth, so are my ways higher than your ways and my thoughts than your thoughts" (Isaiah 55:8-9).

In a moment when our peace is threatened, we should desire to have the very thoughts of God toward us and our situation.

"Robert Louis Stevenson tells of a storm that caught a vessel off a rocky coast and threatened to drive it and its passengers to destruction. In the midst of the terror of the storm, one daring man defied all orders, made a dangerous passage to the pilothouse and saw the Steerman, lashed fast at his post of holding the wheel unwaveringly, and inch by inch, turning the ship out, once more, to sea. The pilot saw the watcher and smiled.

Then, the daring passenger went below and gave out a note of cheer: "I have seen the face of the pilot, and he smiled. All is well."[13]

When we gaze upon the beautiful face of our Lord Jesus Christ in the storms of our lives the superior knowledge of knowing and belonging to Him surpasses our limited understanding of what is happening externally to us and we can proclaim with great cheer as our hearts and minds are guarded in Christ Jesus, that all is well with my soul.

---

[13] https://www.sermonsearch.com/sermon-illustrations/893/he-smiled/

The wisdom of the Lord is far superior.
The Holy Spirit who lives in us will point us
to Christ who is our supply and we can
receive spiritual truth that will guard our
hearts and minds in Christ Jesus.
Adam Clarke said, "Shall keep them as in
a strong place or castle. Your hearts - the
seat of all your affections and passions,
and minds - your understanding,
judgment, and conscience through Christ
Jesus; by whom ye were brought into this
state of favor, through whom ye are
preserved in it, and in whom ye possess
it; for Christ keeps that heart in peace in
which He dwells and rules.
This peace passeth all understanding; it is
of a very different nature from all that can
arise from human occurrences.
It is a peace which Christ has purchased,
and which God dispenses; it is felt by all
the truly godly, but can be explained by
none; it is communion with the Father,
and His Son Jesus Christ, by the power
and influence of the Holy Ghost."[14]

If you continuing reading Philippians 4:8-9
it says, "...whatever things are true,
whatever things are noble, whatever
things are just, whatever things are pure,
whatever things are lovely, whatever

[14] Adam Clarke Commentary.
https://www.studylight.org/commentary/philippians/4-7.html

things are of good report, if there is any virtue and if there is anything praiseworthy—meditate on these things and the conclusion is the God of peace will be with you!

Just as Adam Clarke said, we have been brought into this state of favor, so replace thoughts of worry with thoughts of His unconditional and immeasurable love for you. As we keep meditating on His promises in His Word we are reminded, the God of peace is with us. Thanksgiving flows from our hearts because of Jesus and the blood-bought right we have to His peace, a worry-free mind, and removal of stress as we cast our cares upon Him.

**#4th Reward of Peace: Our hearts and minds will be guarded in Christ Jesus.**

The reward of peace (with God) is the capacity to receive spiritual truth from God that surpasses our limited finite wisdom in all situations that will guard our hearts (affections and passions) and minds (understanding, judgment, conscience) of the favorable position we have in Christ Jesus.

**#5th Reward of Peace:** Citizenship into the Kingdom of Peace.

Philippians 3:20: "But we are citizens of heaven, where the Lord Jesus Christ lives. And we are eagerly waiting for him to return as our Savior."



You have probably heard the expression when someone dies that they are finally at peace.
What the person is saying whether they realize it or not is that for a believer, they have the blessed state of peace that comes with death. When the righteous die they enter into the kingdom of peace.

The kingdom has three main characteristics: righteousness, peace, and joy.

"For the kingdom of God is not a matter of eating and drinking, but of righteousness, peace, and joy in the Holy Spirit" (Romans 14:17).

What might be even more incredible to discover is that the characteristics of the Kingdom are our reality today. Righteousness, peace, and joy are all found in Jesus.

<u>Old Testament Scripture Index</u>
(Page number in parenthesis)

## Old Testament

1. Genesis 1:28 (62)

2. Deuteronomy 28:1-2,6 (44), 28:15 (44)

3. Joshua 1:8 (45)

4. Judges 18:5-6 (41)

5. Psalm 29:11 (49), 34:14 (65)

6. Proverbs 12:1-14 (78), 12:20 (76)

7. Isaiah 11:10 (25), 26:3 (55), 55:8-9 (80), 65:25 (62)

8. Micah 5:5 (63)

<u>New Testament Scripture Index</u>

(Page number in parenthesis)

## The New Testament

1. Matthew 5:9 (70), 5:17 (44), 6:6 (12), 6:20 (75), 9:2 (13), 19:25-26 (19)

2. Luke 2:14 (63)

3. John 14:9 (69), 14:27 (50), 15 (75), 15:5 (72), 16:33 (50)

4. Romans 1:17 (32), 2:6-7 (75), 4:3 (34), 4:13-16 (35), 5:1 (34), 5:2 (36), 8:9-11 (43), 8:31 (40), 14:17 (84), 15:12 (25), 15:13 (18)

5. 1 Corinthians 1:3 (32), 2:16 (80)

6. 2 Corinthians 1:9-10 (21), 5:19 (32)

7. Galatians 3:13 (45)

8. Ephesians 1:6 (32), 2:8-9 (43), 2:12 (21), 4:12 (53)

9. Philippians 1:6 (43), 1:20b-21 (33), 3:20 (83), 4:6-7 (20) (79), 4:8-9 (82), 4:11-13 (33)

10. Colossians 2:13 (32), 3:15 (48), 3:16-17 (54)

11. 1 Thessalonians 5:5 (61)

12. 2 Thessalonians 1:2 (5), 1:3 (18)

13. 2 Timothy 4:17-18 (52)

14. Hebrews 4:15 (58), 4:16 (39), 9:15 (43), 10:4 (32), 12:14 (64)

15. James 3:18 (75)

16. 1 Peter 1:2 (14), 1:15 (68), 2:20,21,23 (70), 3:8-22 (68)

17. 2 Peter 1:2 (14), 1:3 (55)

18. 1 John 3:1-2a (71)

19. Revelation 22 (62), 22:12 (75)

# Some Other Books By Rev. Dr. Matthew Webster

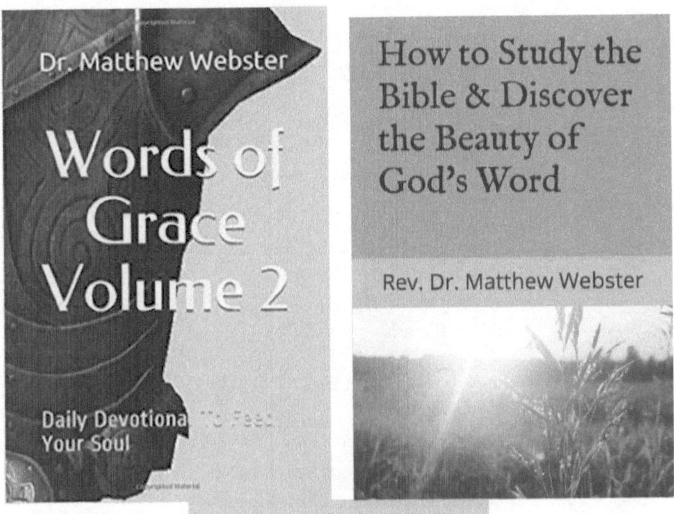

Dr. Webster's entire library can be found at **www.acts433.com**

God Bless You!

Dr. Matthew Webster founded Acts 433
Church in 2015. The goal is to reveal
Jesus so that believers might rest in the
finished work of the Savior as they realize
the freedom over sin and death they have
to respond in victory, reaffirming the good
news of the Gospel of Jesus Christ to the
world. Acts 433 Church through its grace
teaching resources has a vision to become
the largest little church in the world, as we
train leaders how to receive and impart
God's grace and support the development
of micro churches world-wide.